MW01601101

The Last Weekend

A Story of Love, Loss, and Hope

C. B. Schneider

WESTBOW
PRESS®
A DIVISION OF THOMAS NELSON
& ZONDERVAN

Scriptures taken from the Holy Bible, New International Version®, NIV®. Copyright © 1973, 1978, 1984, 2011 by Biblica, Inc.™ Used by permission of Zondervan. All rights reserved worldwide. www.zondervan.com The "NIV" and "New International Version" are trademarks registered in the United States Patent and Trademark Office by Biblica, Inc.

WestBow Press books may be ordered through booksellers or by contacting:

WestBow Press
A Division of Thomas Nelson & Zondervan
1663 Liberty Drive
Bloomington, IN 47403
www.westbowpress.com
1 (866) 928-1240

ISBN: 978-1-9736-5918-1 (sc)
ISBN: 978-1-9736-5920-4 (hc)
ISBN: 978-1-9736-5919-8 (e)

Library of Congress Control Number: 2019904072

Print information available on the last page.

WestBow Press rev. date: 04/12/2019

There are so many people to thank for making this book a reality that I could go on and on; blood family and family friends, you know who you are and how much I love and cherish all of you. My bottom line is to thank God for the vision and the words, and for Bill, my beloved husband, who never stopped believing in me. Ever.

Contents

Introduction

I NEVER THOUGHT I WOULD OUTLIVE MY BELOVED HUSBAND, BILL. I thought we would be one of the few couples to grow old together like bookends, still in love as the decades rolled by. Well, here I am, sixteen months after his unexpected death, and I'm trying to stay focused on learning to breathe again, without him.

If you are reading this, then you may have become a card-holding member of the widow/widower club. Welcome. I wish (just as you do) that we were not in this club; the dues are extreme. Even in this digital age, we can't hit the reset button, no matter how much we want to. There is no do-over.

I want you to know that you're not going crazy. You will have good days, mediocre days, and horrible days ahead. Not gonna lie. Your grief path may be similar to mine; it may also be vastly different. Some of the thoughts I've documented in my new journey may cause you to cry, laugh, just nod your head, or all of these. We're the same but different. We're widows/widowers in a digital age who will have to fight with every ounce of our being to be able to fix our digital lives for ourselves and our family.

You're lonely but not alone. Take a deep breath. Take another one. And take one more. Learn to breathe deeply again.

God is with you.
C. B. Schneider
August 13, 2018

April 2017

NO ONE EVER TELLS YOU HOW TO BE A WIDOW; SOMETIMES, IT JUST happens out of the blue. My Saturday blue sky brought instant widowhood without warning, without any promises, and without my best friend for the rest of my life here on this earth. In thirty minutes on April 29, 2017, my world came crashing down, and I knew my life would never be the same.

My husband was one of those healthy individuals who gets a cold, is sick for one day, and is 100 percent better the next day. Super annoying. I would then get the cold and be down and out for a week or more, sniffing, coughing, using up all the Kleenex in the house. Bill was a happy person, always cheerful in the morning. My rule was "Don't talk to me until I talk to you; you are safe once I talk to you." He was the reason I got up each morning and went to bed with him each night. He was my safety, my rock, my love, my other half, and the father to our daughter, Kristen. He was Daddy. He was the one who could soothe her nerves, the fail-safe car fixer, the manual reader of the house. If it was electronic, he not only understood it but also would install it and teach you how to use it. He was the handyman of the house. We planned for now, and we tried to save for the future that we thought we would have with each other. Undiagnosed heart disease and a massive heart attack proved both of us wrong just five months shy of our thirtieth wedding anniversary.

BILL AND CHRIS SCHNEIDER, SEPTEMBER 25, 1987

The beauty of our relationship meant that we talked about everything and nothing. We had discussions about death. We both knew that we didn't want to continue life if either of us were hooked up to a machine keeping our physical forms alive. We agreed that the surviving spouse should go on and find love again. I remember these conversations as if they happened yesterday. We were so filled with love for each other. We thought these conversations were unreal, but we still had them, together.

I have provided a discussion form (see appendix) as a way to start a conversation together. These conversations are really important! If you don't have a living will, you will need your surviving spouse to know your wishes.

We both wanted to be cremated for a number of reasons, one being that we didn't want to purchase land just to be buried in it. We viewed land as something to use or invest in when you're alive or provide as an inheritance. You don't own anything once you're dead. While this would give the survivor(s) a place to visit, it wasn't something that either of us wanted for the other. Also, it's easier to visit his urn that has found its place in the living room. I still have him with me every day; this gives me peace. Having a burial plot is your decision, and you need to do what is right for you and your spouse. Honor what the two of you decide, no one else. Many people born before 1960 or so may have already purchased their side-by-side plots somewhere serene and beautiful. This is a great way to provide peace of mind to those left behind. I can see the beauty of owning such plots. This is your life and your death; do what makes you happy.

Bill and I had been pretty busy the month of April 2017. Our weekends were filled with commitments we'd made to friends— first a weekend of filming a cable show and then a weekend getaway to Duluth, Minnesota, with three other amazing couples (our total was eight people). It was a fabulous weekend filled with friendship, food, hiking, rock hunting, all-day Jenga games, and (cleansed) Cards Against Humanity. There was a double rainbow on Lake Superior. I managed to catch a picture of just one of the rainbows from our deck.

ONE RAINBOW, LAKE SUPERIOR, DULUTH, MINNESOTA

Bill's turn at Jenga

C. B. SCHNEIDER

BILL AND SOME OF THE GROUP HIKING

If I had known this was the last weekend I'd have with Bill, I would have told him repeatedly how much I loved him, how much I needed him, and that he was the best part of my life. I saw this rainbow as the simple promise of God's love that He has always provided for everyone.

By Saturday, April 29, we had a number of things to do at our Elm Street house and a few errands to run. Our dog, Frodo, had a haircut appointment, two cars had license tags due, and we had to get some yardwork done. Bill absolutely disliked dandelions in his lawn. There were a few alive and well in the grass, and he was on a mission to eradicate them that day. Bill dropped off Frodo, got the tabs and weed killer, and then came home to wake me by playing music. But I was already up and dressed for a partial day of yardwork.

Bill sprayed the weeds while I cleaned up a mugo pine bush in the front of the house. I was lying on the ground, determining which branch to saw off, as the branches twist all around inside, and I needed to make sure that the bush was getting enough air. Bill told me he had heartburn and went into the house to get some antacids and a bottle of water. Looking back on this part now, perhaps heartburn should have been a signal to me. We had gone to a buffet in Blaine, Minnesota, the previous Wednesday. He'd had heartburn that night, but that was normal for him. He could get heartburn from water. His mother, Betty, had had heartburn all the time from just about anything. So I didn't get worried. But I wish I had.

Bill's heartburn that Wednesday night had gotten him out of bed, and he'd slept on the couch, half sitting up. Oh, if I could hit the reset button, I would have taken him to the hospital that night! If only I had known how bad his heartburn might have been; if he had just told me it was worse than normal. Maybe he hadn't known either. I wonder if he'd had a minor heart attack that night. I will never know. I could play the what-if game for the rest of my life, but I'm not sure I could have helped change what happened. I have to forgive myself for not knowing.

Once Bill took antacids, he came back outside with a bottle of water. As he walked toward me, I looked at him. His face was white, and he was not walking right. He told me he didn't feel well. That was the last thing he said to me. Ever. I got up from under the bush and rushed toward him. He hit the ground, dropping the water bottle. I grabbed his arm. He managed to get up, and I dialed 911 as we walked toward the garage. I think I was trying to get him into my car. I really don't remember what I was thinking at that moment. Adrenaline had kicked in, and I was in fight mode.

Once in the garage, he fell toward my car, hit it, and rolled to the back of the garage by the workbench. He was not speaking, foam was coming out of his mouth, and he was lying on his side. I tried to get him on his back, screaming at 911 to come and help me since I was not able to move him to his back. I set the phone on the garage floor and tried to cradle his head and turn him onto his back.

At some point, I began to cry uncontrollably, pleading, "Please don't leave me! I need you!"

I knew in my heart that he was already leaving me, and there was nothing I could do to stop this horrible nightmare from taking its course.

Oh, Bill! You are my life, my love. Please don't leave me. I don't want to go through life without you!

911 Emergency Network

IF YOU HAVE TO CALL THE 911 EMERGENCY NETWORK FOR AN AMBULANCE, know that in order to get out of the "lock" of the network, you will need to reboot your phone. The 911 network locks on your cellphone in order to make sure to find where you are calling from. I had *no* idea that I was locked onto this network when I found out where the ambulance was going to take my husband. I tried to call my daughter; she could not hear me. I sent her texts—many of them failed—a few ended up getting through to her.

Once the hospital was known, and I texted her, I was being driven to that hospital by one of the police. It was one of the longest car rides of my entire life. I sent a few texts out to my mom and to Kelley while I was waiting. Kristen tried multiple times to call me; I answered the phone, but she could not hear me at all. I could hear her. How useful is this? I can understand the validity of the lock in the network, but, at some point, release the lock, okay? Remember that the surviving spouse can't possibly think straight to even begin to realize that his or her phone is locked into the 911 network.

Once I arrived at the hospital, my phone was still not functioning properly. The officer who drove me there stayed with me for a while. The ER staff took me back to a room and told me that while Bill was still hooked up to machines, this action was not promising. I knew then that he was going to die. I asked them to leave him attached to the machines until Kristen arrived. She would need to see that they were trying everything to keep him alive. The nurse left the room and came back to tell me that this was not possible; Bill was gone. He had given up his spirit and was now beginning his own journey toward heaven. My heart was broken, and I was in shock and complete disbelief. Silent tears flowed down my face uncontrollably.

Oh, God, please help me! How can I live this live without him? I don't want to be alone!

The nurse brought me back to another room, where his body was laid out on a cold, metal table. I knew in my heart that Bill's soul had passed out of this physical world and only his shell was laying on the table. Kristen still had not arrived, and I was in the midst of disbelief and unreality. At some point, Kristen was brought into the sterile room where he was laying. We hugged and sobbed uncontrollably together. Not sure who was holding who up at that moment. Our world had tipped sideways, and the floor was not steady for either of us.

We cried and said goodbye to Bill, my love and her dad. I brushed his cold check. I really wanted to lie down on the table next to him, put his arms around me one last time, and to kiss him goodbye. I didn't think this was a good idea since Kristen was in the room. I'm still sorry to this day that I didn't do this before she arrived. Oh, for one more moment of time to be in his arms and kiss him! I simply walked toward his belongings in the plastic hospital bag, and together Kristen and I walked out of the room. I didn't look back. This was one of the first difficult actions that I had to force myself to do that day—and for weeks afterward. *I can't believe you're gone! My love! Why?*

Tears were flowing freely down both of our faces. We were stopped before we opened the door and brought back to the first room I'd originally been in and a female pastor was brought to the room to talk to us. Both of us were sad and crying, but we knew that his spirit had gone to heaven. I believe she was amazed at the peace (despite our red faces and streaming tears) we showed her in this specific regard. Even in my grief-laden fog, I recognized this and held onto this moment in my heart.

We were allowed to leave after I'd signed my name a few times. As we walked out of the U of M Hospital, I realized that I was a widow. I walked a block away from the hospital and dropped my purse. I wanted to sink to the concrete and cry with all my might. Instead, I asked Kristen for her phone since mine was nonfunctional. She searched for Sandy, one of Bill's sisters, dialed, and handed me her phone. This was another unrealistic moment in my life, telling one of three sisters that their (favorite) only brother had just died.

Kristen drove us to the house I shared with Bill, her childhood home. It was a scary ride; she shouldn't have been driving, but we didn't have a choice. I called Angie, using Kristen's phone, to tell her about Bill as well, and then called Jean. When we arrived, Jean, Craig, Bailee, and Blake were already at our house. The first of the family began to arrive. At some point in time, more family and friends started to arrive, just like the never-ending food supply that multiplied like rabbits. I thought about the fishes and loaves of bread that Jesus had multiplied and fed thousands in a second of lucidity and logic. I know I was in a daze, still crying, in disbelief, feeling as if I was holding my breath or I was breathing too shallowly.

Unless you reboot your phone, it will not function well.

C. B. SCHNEIDER

You have to get off the emergency network in order to talk to your family and friends. Despite grief and disbelief, you need to remember this or hope that someone will help you remember. I must have rebooted my phone at some point on April 29, 2017, because a flurry of texts and calls were then coming in and the person calling could hear me. I was in the garage most of the night, crying and talking with friends. I felt that I had to face the garage like a warrior to be able to get over being in the place where he'd had his heart attack. Many people were there for Kristen and I, telling us they would help take care of things (house and yard) and to not worry about anything. Kelley, Brett, and Palmer peeps were there, with food and love from the Palmer House in Sauk Centre, Minnesota. Kelley and Brett were staying as long as Kristen and I needed them. The Elm Street house was full of people and food—but not my beloved husband in physical form. I didn't know how to handle the that moment, or the next.

I can't believe you're gone! I want you back with me! How can this happen?

Donor Call

I TOOK THE CALL FROM THE DONOR ORGANIZATION LATER IN THE afternoon of the first day, advising them where to deliver Bill's body when they were done and trying to answer the woman on the other end of the line as clearly and succinctly as I could about Bill's health history, since he was a donor and I knew the importance of the call. I put on my business persona and just dealt with it. You can override the wishes of your loved one at any time—when the call comes the same day; however, this is a call that you can't put off until you can think straight. It's either you take the call while the organs and tissue are still viable and useful, or you override and say no. Not a whole lot of choice in this situation for me.

You can become a donor when you renew your driver's license. Bill's eyes ended up being donated, and this makes my soul happy. I wholeheartedly encourage everyone to become a donor, as Bill was, and I am too. You will be giving the gift of a better life for someone else in this world.

I don't remember much more about that day. It was an

enormous blur. I think Kristen and I did try to sleep that first night. Most of the night, all I could think about was the death scene that I had experienced in the garage. And the tear faucet that would not shut off, no matter how hard I tried to make it stop. I just couldn't believe what had happened that day. Shock, disbelief, and anguish were my new best friends. My heart was heavy with sadness. My widow fog was like the weight of the world on my shoulders. I just couldn't believe what was going on. I just existed from one moment to the next.

I do remember my mom arriving from Florida on Sunday, the next day. There was more crying, eating, and coffee. More friends stopped by, and the fridge was so full we had food on all of the counters. I distinctly remember managing to email my boss on my iPhone (through my tears) about not being in for a while due to Bill's unexpected death. I knew he wouldn't get this email until Monday, but I took care of it when I remembered to that second day. I tried to remember to text my friend Marion; but sadness took over, or I had to greet someone visiting, and I forgot to send this text. Do what you need to do when you remember it! (No matter what time it is: trust me!) You will be glad in the long run that you took the time to do whatever it was that your brain remembered. Widow fog is real and can last for months.

As Monday unfolded, I logged in to my work laptop and sent off a few emails and set my email to out-of-office. I forwarded emails to colleagues, who by now, I hoped, had found out about Bill's death. A few coworkers told me I was strong because who in the world would be thinking about work right now? And there I was, making sure that my colleagues had the latest info and status to take over my work. I thought this was just a normal part of work life and something I had to do in order to not cause issues for my colleagues. This was not strong; it was my brief moment of normalcy and survival. Thank you to those who told me I was strong. Even though my heart was broken and my life had been turned upside down, hearing that I was a strong person encouraged me at that moment.

I had to call Bill's boss and tell him that Bill wouldn't be in the office today, or ever. Oh, the pain of making this call! I tried my best to keep from crying, but I know I failed. Epically. The next time I heard from the company, the CEO phoned to express her condolences, and then HR. This phenomenal company was a bright spot in my journey, helping me with information that I didn't have, and they were incredibly supportive to this new widow. A heartfelt thank-you does not express my appreciation for all of your support of my beloved Bill.

CHAPTER

4

Funeral Planning

I WILL TELL YOU THIS PART IS MORE DIFFICULT THAN YOU CAN imagine. You now have to deal with other people who really don't give a crap that you just lost the love of your life. The funeral home does a *great* job working with grieving people; however, there are others who can be a real pill. To others, this is just a normal day for them. For you, it is the first week of your new life, you are in shock, anguish, and disbelief. I felt like I could not breathe.

Remember: no one knows the road you walk or how your shoes fit during this time. I know you will want to scream at everyone, "Don't you know my husband/wife just died?" You wonder why they can't see it on your face or in your eyes or in your body language. People don't know unless you share this with them. Know that most people don't know what to say, and they end up saying the wrong thing—even though their intents might be good. Until you have experienced loss in this physical life, you simply don't know the devastation of losing your spouse, and words can be so cheap. You will *know* who really shares in your pain and those who can only share it on the surface or say the "right" perfunctory statement. Remember that people are doing their best to be there for you.

Once you pick the funeral home, you will need to meet with the funeral director and make some of the first decisions that are important for you and your family. Have your family close and include very close friends if you believe it will help you. I did, and I wouldn't have been able to make the decisions I made without everyone being there for me and Kristen. You will decide what the obituary says, when it will be posted, and what newspaper it will be printed in. Note: you may need this as a document later to prove your beloved's death. I cut it out of the newspaper and took a digital photo of it. This simple act saved me time during the first few months.

You will decide the program, the pallbearers, the songs, the order of the service. You will need to determine who will perform the service. Whether or not this ends up to be you doing the eulogy, this is 100 percent up to you as the final decision-maker. Suggestions are good, but don't do anything that you don't want to or that would not be right for your spouse. As we were not officially affiliated with a specific church, I chose to perform the eulogy. Who better than his best friend and wife? I felt that this was the right thing to do, and I knew that if this was what I had to do, then God would give me the strength to do it. I did have someone lead a prayer. Even though he was to be cremated, I wanted to have pallbearers, his best friend Brett and his nephews, to stand up in front of everyone at the service while the last song played.

If you are cremating your spouse, you will need to select the urn or urns and the casket. I selected a simple silver urn and two small silver hearts for Kristen and me in record time, apparently. I walked in, viewed what was available, and settled on silver urns immediately. This was not difficult at all. Family had me look again at all the urns to make sure of my decision. I glanced around the room, but still came to my original decision. I believe this might be hard for others, but making decisions (good or bad) was not my problem right now. Sadness, disbelief, and shock were my problems.

In Minnesota, for cremation, you can rent the outside casket for the service. The insert is what holds your loved one and can be burned, and this is what you pay for. If you choose a burial, choose the casket that best represents your loved one; you will know which one is best for your spouse. Work with the funeral director, as this person will be the best one to provide you with the guidance you will need for burial or for cremation. This is what funeral directors do! This is their job, and you can lean on them.

I do know that there are things that would need to be done if you are burying a loved one in a cemetery or at Fort Snelling or another military service cemetery. Your funeral director will be the best person for you to work with. If you already have a family plot, a call will need to be made to make the land ready and for all the flowers to be brought to the funeral. Rely on the funeral director and staff to do things that you don't know how to do or what you should do. The director will be clear about his role and your role.

Flowers for the Funeral

If you have a favorite flower shop already, go there and look at the books that show you casket sprays first. Then work with the designer. I do want to tell you that this is *your* decision; don't let someone else dictate to you what you should do. There shouldn't be hard and fast rules to a flower arrangement—even if you want colors that do not look good together. Who really cares about something like that at this point in time? Huh? Seriously, it's not about the creation of a perfect floral arrangement. It's about what you want for your spouse.

My husband was a very humble man—someone who would rather be behind the camera taking pictures rather than the front man in charge of the event. He didn't want to be the center of attention; he liked to fade into the background and watch the shenanigans and capture them with his camera. He did like to create shenanigans and point to me as the person to blame for them. It was all in fun. So I wanted flowers that were subdued, not too many, and ones that truly represented him. Sunflowers always reminded me of Bill, because of his cheerful personality, but he always gave me roses. My favorites are sterling roses, which are light purple and have a beautiful citrus smell, but are hard to find, and rather expensive. I didn't want to be extravagant; Bill would not like this for himself at all.

I chose one red rose from me to signify our love, and Kristen selected a pink rose which ended up being somewhat of a melon color due to the designer's opinion of red and pink together not looking nice and her attitude in general about the whole job of working with me. My need had interrupted her day and created more work for her. I wanted to ask her, "Whose casket spray is this? Yours? Thanks for your opinion, but I really don't care when you say it as if I am making your day difficult!"

I screamed this in my head while I managed a smile at her through my tears. I wanted to rip her head off, but I refrained. Thank you, Bill, for being there with me during something that should have been easy and simple. Instead, this was my first people/business-related horrible experience on day four, and an unfortunate eye-opener of things to come.

We had a few purple flowers for balance, and the rest was white daisies, calla lilies, and greenery.

Bill was someone special to everyone. To capture his life with ribbons, he was son, son-in-law, husband, dad, uncle, godfather, nephew, and friend. I required all eight of these titles to be included in the spray to honor him. I wanted *white* ribbons with the titles in gold. Make sure you point out what *you* mean by *white*. His spray was made with *opaque* "white" with gold letters. This was not my vision, and the designer's interrupted day meant she decided what I meant rather than asking me about it. I found out this is "normal" for the floral company.

Personally, make sure that you are having a meeting of the minds so that you end up with what you envisioned. Make sure you point out everything you want, even if the designer you are working with does not ask you what you mean. I have just impacted her day with my needs, and she was not too happy about providing customer service. Either you love your job, or you need to find something else to do. Life is way too short!

Picture Boards

IF YOU HAVE PEOPLE WHO HAVE PICTURES, LET THEM BE IN CHARGE of making their own picture boards. You may or may not be up to helping to do this—and that is okay. If this is what you love to do, then take control and advise others on what you want. Explain your vision and needs and accept the help that people want to provide to you.

Your family and friends have no idea of how to be helpful to you. They are suffering just as much as you are right now. Don't be a dictator about this. Just let them have free rein if you want. I did, and it was such a wonderfully freeing action not to have to make decisions about which pictures to use, how many boards, the design and presentation, and who should do what.

I have three of the most incredible sisters-in-law that anyone could ask for. They all did what they wanted, and I loved them for sharing their pictures and memories of their brother the way they wanted. Don't get me wrong; I love picture boards, and I enjoy looking at them. I just don't want to make them. (Not in my wheelhouse.)

CHAPTER

6

Music

THERE ARE SO MANY SONGS THAT YOU CAN CHOOSE FROM, AND THE funeral home will already have songs to select from; and your family and friends will provide suggestions. Go with your heart and choose what best represents your spouse.

I chose "Live Like That" by Sidewalk Prophets as the signal for the service to begin and "I Can Only Imagine" by Mercy Me for the ending song. Bill, Kristen, and I loved the song by Mercy Me, and all three of us would sing along with this one in the car or in church when we heard it. It's a song of uplifting glory that clearly spells out what our belief for someone's passing from this life to the next phase, since we can only imagine what one would see and the joy felt upon reaching heaven and seeing the Father for the first time.

If you choose to listen to Sidewalk Prophets' song, "Live Like That," you will have heard a musical representation of the man my husband was in this physical life. I selected it while everyone was out of the house and I was alone for the first time. I listened to it and cried my eyes out, when the song came to "when I'm home where my soul belongs" and "when they see me, do they see You?"

Yes, Bill. Everything you said and did showed the glory of God to those who met you and became your friend. You lived like that. I am just your humble wife, best friend, and partner in crime. You were my soulmate, best friend, and lover. I still have trouble living this life without you. I miss you every single day that we have been apart. You're the reason that I am who I am—then and now. You encouraged me to be who I am and what I am like no one else ever did. You supported me through college and grad school by taking the household chores off my shoulders and gently pushing me forward.

I love you and miss you, Bill. How am I supposed to go on in this life without you?

Eulogy

I GAVE THE EULOGY AT MY HUSBAND'S GOING-HOME CELEBRATION (funeral). From my vantage point, the room was packed to overflowing capacity. There wasn't an empty seat in the room; people were sitting and standing in the room as well as in the entryway. This was the true representation of who Bill was in this physical life. He touched hundreds of people in different ways with his love and servant attitude.

I am going to share with all of you my prayer from this past Monday morning, the third day of my new life.

Good Morning, Father:

I know that you have a plan for my life
as it states in Jeremiah 29:11:

"'For I know the plans I have for you,' declares the Lord, 'plans to prosper you and not to harm you, plans to give you hope and a future.'"

Father, I know you are very much aware of the sorrow that my family is facing right now; you have experienced it as well with the death of your own Son. When the sorrow of Bill's passing hits me like a wave, please help me to lean on you for the strength needed to ride that wave to get to the safe shores of your endless love.

I ask for comfort and strength for my family and all those who loved Bill. I know that he is with you and those loved ones who have gone before us to be with you forever in heaven; I think of his mom specifically, your servant, Betty. I can only imagine the glorious reunion that has happened already and will continue in heaven. This gives me the comfort and strength needed to get through this human life without the love of my life. Amen.

Bill was an amazing person; he was humble, a true servant of God. He was able to make everyone around him feel loved, safe, and protected. He was my best friend; we could talk about everything for hours on end and not realize how much time has passed. He was my counselor, my sounding board, my protector, my love. He was also the reason I had coffee in the morning, lawn care, and vehicle maintenance. This was his joke to me.

Bill was a fabulous father. He was the one who first cared for Kristen when she was born, holding her like a football, changing her, feeding her. His abilities in this area amazed (and ticked off) the nurses, since they were not able to teach him. Father and daughter shared a bond that was unshakeable, a true, pure love that was not just reserved for her, but truly radiated out from his eyes and his whole being. Bill is an organ donor, and my hope was that someone would be able to receive his eyes. I am pleased to say that his eyes have been donated. Hopefully, that person will be able to see as Bill has seen life and love and the beauty of watching his daughter grow up.

Bill's family was the backbone of his world. He would do anything for his parents, his sisters, or his aunts and uncles. His love for them and his servant nature was boundless, especially for his nieces and nephews and his friends. He was the most positive and cheerful morning person you would have ever met. Even though Kristen and I loved him dearly, his cheerful morning routine was almost too much for us non-morning people, as Kristen will tell you about later.

Bill was a friend to many. He was an extrovert in one way and an introvert in another. His house was his sanctuary, and his church was his family, friends, and nature. He had an amazing eye for unique pictures that he saw in everyday life. He was able to read people like a book before they said anything. He was a nonjudgmental person—his goal was to love you where you were at in life, no matter what, no matter what you had done, and help you if he could.

Bill was the wind beneath my wings 100 percent. When I enrolled in college to finish my BA and eventually my master's, he was right there cheering me on, cleaning the house, and taking care of business. This was true love. He was the reason I reached these goals during our twenty-nine years together. His mother once told me before we were married in 1987 that I was the "right woman to kick him in his rear." He was not a wallflower. He was a calm and loving person who needed someone here on earth to push him to his full potential. I have been deeply honored to be that person for him.

There are no words to express my level of sorrow in saying goodbye to my husband, my love. I know it is difficult for everyone in this room to grasp the magnitude of his passing. I can only go with the fact that I know where his soul is right now—he is home where his soul belongs, at the feet of the Father, laying down his crown and praising Him.

I would like to ask someone to lead us all in the Lord's Prayer.

Now I would like to share the reading of Ecclesiastes chapter three, verses one through eight, prior to opening up the podium for anyone to share a story or something special about Bill.

There is a time for everything, and a season for every activity under heaven:

A time to be born and a time to die,

A time to plant and a time to uproot,

A time to kill and a time to heal,

A time to tear down and a time to build,

A time to weep and a time to laugh,

A time to mourn and a time to dance,

A time to scatter stones and a time to gather them,

A time to embrace and a time to refrain,

A time to search and a time to give up,

A time to keep and a time to throw away,

A time to tear and a time to mend,

A time to be silent and a time to speak,

A time to love and a time to hate,

A time for war and a time for peace.

I have chosen the song "Live Like That" by Sidewalk Prophets as this is truly the musical version of Bill's life. He would be here telling all of you that you should not be sad for him; rather, celebrate his life, your relationship with him, and live like that. He was a walking sermon for God's love for everyone.

I invite anyone to share in your love and remembrance of Bill. Kristen will speak first, and then, please, share your memories of Bill for everyone to hear.

I get that others may have a religious person perform this part of the service, and either way is neither right nor wrong. You need to do what feels best for you and is representative of your spouse. I believed I needed to perform this service, and I told everyone, "I got this."

I can't tell you how many people came up to me and told me

that I would not be able to do this and that I should have someone else speak about Bill for me. I just smiled and thanked them for their concern. I *knew* that God would be there to give me the courage to stand before the overflowing crowd and talk about the man I loved with all my heart. I *never* doubted God's plan for the day of Bill's funeral and have never doubted that there was a reason for his death.

I wish I had known that he'd had heart disease! I would have made sure that this was taken care of somehow. This physical life ended for Bill, and his soul was returned to heaven. I don't have to like it—this was not what I wanted or what I had envisioned for us—but I am not in charge of the universe. I have to accept this fact.

I'm learning to breathe again, not as shallowly as the first few days, but better.

C. B. SCHNEIDER

The Celebration Luncheon

FROM MY EXPERIENCE, DON'T PLAN ON EATING AT ALL. IT'S NOT MUCH different than our wedding. Were you able to eat? Did anyone give you the time to do this? Everyone is happy and wants a part of your time during the happy event. It's the same when you are hosting a celebration of life, a going-home party, as it is being a bride or groom at a wedding. Truly, do what you need to do: if you need to eat, then make sure you eat. If you don't, just take a plate and try to eat.

You probably won't be hungry anyway. You'll be going through the motions of eating to make others happy and feel good. There will be so many people to talk to you'll be lucky to get a cup of coffee or a glass of water. This is okay. Do what you need to do. No one should be telling you what to do or how to act either. Your family and friends will be concerned about you, so try to eat even if you can't right then. There is always later in the day when you can concentrate on eating or when you feel/want to eat.

If you are the consummate planner and love to figure out

the best luncheon food, how much, and so on, then you go for it! This is *not* what I am good at. For the family holidays, there is a set meal, and I was instructed what to bring. This is *perfect* for me. I really don't like to cook or plan food. I was floundering with this task—it was *so* clear to everyone except me. I thought I had to take care of everything!

Kelley gently reminded me that this was what she was very good at. Kelley took this over for me, and I gave her a budget that was probably too low. I admit I really was not thinking straight about this. I decided to stick to writing the eulogy, as this was what I really wanted to do and what I knew *was* in my wheelhouse. Give up the reins whenever someone tells you that they "got this" for you. Let others take care of you and you can concentrate on what you need to concentrate on. This is not a sign of weakness; this is the love and care that others are trying to show/give you in your hour of need. Allowing others to help makes them feel needed. Others' shoulders can handle what you can't or don't want to. Just ask for help! This does not make you weak. It shows you are strong.

What ended up happening was perfect under the guiding hands of Kelley and her staff from the Palmer House Hotel, Restaurant, and Pub in Sauk Centre, Minnesota. All of the staff were not only there for the service for Bill, but also they served and took care of all of the people who came to the luncheon. I love the PH staff. They have always been, and forever will be, my family and friends.

It never dawned on me that for the PH staff to be at Bill's funeral, they had to close the PH for the day. Duh. Note: this is a reminder that you will have widow fog. This is a true example of family friends and love like none other.

Know that you will be having guests at your house after the celebration luncheon. I asked my PH family to come to my house so that I could share more of my life with Bill. The staff had only seen Bill and me at the PH; I wanted to share more about Bill with them before the day was truly over. I needed their presence and their love. One of the stories that I shared about our life was the basement construction. We did most of the construction ourselves, from framing to painting. On a wall outside of the room that would become our bedroom, my shenanigan-loving husband painted "Bill (heart) Chris" on the wall and let it dry. He asked me to come see something, and as I turned the corner to find out what he wanted me to see.

First thought, so sweet! Second thought, spoken out loud, "Bill! You need to paint over that! Dad will come down here and not be happy about that!"

Literally, the words had *just* come out of my mouth when

my dad came down the stairs, turned the corner, and told Bill he needed to paint over his scribbling. Despite many coats of paint, if you look at just the right angle, you can still see it on the wall today. Words scribbled over seventeen years ago are still there to proclaim the love we shared. It made a great story for the new owners of the house when I sold it, and they plan to do the same thing somewhere in the house to keep their story of love just as strong.

In 2004, in Arizona, I found a metal heart with an arrow through it. I thought this was a perfect item to hang on the wall that Bill had painted his love on. I mimicked his scribbling in the sign and gave it to him for Christmas. This sign had been hanging on the same wall for thirteen years.

Other family members were there as well for the continuation of the celebration, and we shared stories and memories of Bill. It was a beautiful day in early May, and we opened the garage doors to welcome in the warm breeze while we sat in a circle to see one another, laughing at stories and crying over the memories.

All too soon, the celebration was over, and I knew it was back to the real world, where Bill was no longer physically by my side, solving technical issues, or coloring Kristen's hair. I would no longer be able to touch him or feel his touch. My heart was broken, aching in ways that I didn't want to speak aloud. I just wanted him back at my side.

I miss you! I don't want to do this without you! Why, God? Why?

The Enormity of It All– Widowhood

> Pretend you are in mourning. Dress in mourning clothes, and don't use any cosmetic lotions. Act like a woman who has spent many days grieving for the dead.
>
> —2 Samuel 14:2

IF I THOUGHT I KNEW THE TERM *WIDOW* AFTER BILL DIED, I TRULY learned what it meant when I went to bed each night or when I got up each morning. I have discovered, through this journey, that the word *widow* or *widower,* to others, is a harsh word. I didn't have to pretend I was in mourning. I could barely make it out of bed. I still felt like I couldn't breathe deeply. As if I were too scared to do so.

For a while, Kristen and I (and Frodo) shared a bedroom because every room in the house was full, and Kelley and Brett were on the couch upstairs. After sleeping next to Bill for over twenty-nine years, a queen-sized bed becomes larger than life when it's just you and a dog. I cried into Frodo's fur night after night, trying to sleep in the bed we shared. At some point, I had to give Frodo a bath because the salt from my tears made his fur stiff. My loneliness and sadness had no words, just tears.

Frodo was a rescue that had become part of the family in 2008. Just as we had rescued him, it would be Frodo that would rescue me after Bill's death. His love and comfort have meant the world to me. He is my companion, my emotional support animal. I had him certified in order to go places with me. The love of a dog doesn't replace your spouse, but his devotion keeps me going every day. How could you not love that adorable face?

FRODO, THE RESCUE DOG

For years—not even sure how many total—Bill woke up first and took the dog(s) out. The rule was, don't talk to me before my first cup of coffee or until I talked to you. He was the most cheerful and talkative person first thing in the morning, which drove me crazy. I couldn't think until the caffeine kicked in and I'd proclaimed myself civil. Funny how the little things are what you miss the most when your spouse dies unexpectedly. I'm now in charge of letting Frodo out and getting my own coffee. I've become the cheerful person in the morning, now wanting to talk to my daughter or make her coffee. I'm sure Bill is looking down from heaven, smiling and shaking his head. Never, in this physical life did I *ever* think that I would become the early riser *and* be cheerful.

Thanks, my love, for all the years that you were this for me so that I can now be more like you. I still miss you with all my heart! Learning to take a few deep breaths.

> Even in laughter the heart may ache, and joy may end in grief.
>
> —Proverbs 14:13

Bill's Antics

BILL WOKE ME UP EACH SATURDAY OR SUNDAY WITH HIS MUSICAL selections. He was the early riser and would then decide when I had to get up so that we could spend time together by working on whatever the weekend brought. He started with whatever he thought would get me out of bed, with me dancing all the way to meet him in the basement living room.

Oh, I so miss you and all of the fun, silly, and wonderful things you did to make me happy. How can I live this life without you in it? I am so lost and alone without you. I don't want to be without you! I wish there were a life reset button.

Kristen decided to move in with me after Bill died. I was grateful, and I'm still grateful that she is living with me, even though I was initially worried about the cat and the dog residing under the same roof. They've decided to exist under the same roof as long as the "right" owner pets the "right" animal. Fur has not flown as of this writing, even when I do pet the cat. Owners and animals have adjusted nicely to living together in the same space.

Many books have been written about death of a loved one; however, I initially did search for one (and didn't look very hard either) to talk about the death of a father when there's an adult child involved. For all the authors and books out there, sorry! I just couldn't concentrate on finding one when I couldn't even manage to take a shower each day, let alone put on makeup or remember to eat. I was simply trying to exist each day in my newly shattered world.

I was so deep in my own lost-husband grief that I didn't know the right words to say to the daughter who was loved to the moon and back by her dad. I would calmly listen to her and try to think about her grief by taking my own living father out of the picture in my head. While this was a noble thought, I just couldn't grasp her reality. The list of things she thought about now that Bill was gone: Who would take care of our technology, who would fix her car, and who would walk her down the aisle when she got married?

It was the last thought that broke my heart to pieces! I realized that this was not going to be easy but, in fact, would require others helping out both of us for the things we took for granted about our lives. Neither of us ever thought of a world without Bill. I had to help her through her grief, no matter what and no matter who I needed to find for her to talk to. She is my representation of Bill; the most beautiful part of his soul is also part of hers. I am truly blessed to be her mom and her friend.

There's no way that her father can be replaced, and there's no expectation that this is necessary for her or required by me. We have a long list of uncles, cousins, and guy friends who are happy to step up to the plate to help with tasks that Bill used to manage for his girls. For this, I am grateful, thankful, and blessed.

When I do need help, I've learned to step up to the plate to ask for help. I no longer think that asking for help shows weakness. I have reviewed my skills wheelhouse and found that I'm not the most handy-around-the-house person, unless it comes to cleaning. I realize that this has to do with my upbringing and the fact that Bill learned to do quite a bit around the house so that his girls did not. We were princesses without being entitled. We were taken care of by an amazing man, and we were very blessed.

Anger

THERE IS ONE FEELING IN THE PATH OF GRIEF THAT NEITHER KRISTEN nor I experienced, and that is anger. Remember the previous story about the pastor at the U of M Hospital? I believe she was amazed that neither of us were angry about Bill's passing. We were in the first stage of grief, sadness and disbelief, and this makes sense for anyone experiencing an unexpected death of a loved one. I simply was not angry with God then or now.

I don't have to like my new life; I have to adjust to my new life and navigate my way through it. I have to go through the daily sorrow of missing him—whether this is a wave of sadness or just a beautiful memory that makes me smile. You need to go through your own grief. Let the tears run down your face like little prayers; it's a cleansing act. Your new normal equals not knowing when this will happen to you. It can be the most random thing that makes you smile, cry, laugh, scream, or just want to curl up in a ball and go back to bed. All of these feelings can come over you in a minute. I really wasn't sure how sane I was in the beginning of my widowhood because of the rapid-fire way emotions can grab you and send you over the edge.

If you're going through anger, then you need to find the best way to get the anger out of your system. Anger can help you clean your house, cut the grass, or do anything that needs to get done. What anger can't do is rule your new life. You're allowed to be angry at God, the world, or the actions of another if that is what you need to do. You just can't live there.

Anger is a B&B that you visit. It's that simple, really. Since anger is a part of the grief process, you may find it creeping back into your new life at random times, just like the wave that happens when you realize your spouse will not be coming home tonight.

Anger is a chapter in your new book of life, and you need to read it, understand it, and then move to the next chapter. Even if you have to do this every day for the next year, realize this and make sure you also talk to others about these feelings. You just can't live the rest of your life in the state of anger.

Unreality and Disbelief

Oh, THIS TAKES THE WIND RIGHT OUT OF YOUR PROVERBIAL SAILS. These are some of the horrendous waves that I experienced from day one to about month four and beyond. It is the unreality of watching Bill die that first awful day, to finding it hard to believe after thirty years of being with the same person that he is simply not here on this earth anymore.

This is also the utter sadness of my new life that I really had a terrible time with. This sadness can bring you to "Why am I still here?" and "I don't want to go on without him!" How can I? It is too hard, and this is not what I thought my life would be right now, at this age, this time, where we are financially. I thought we still had years of being together; he was the one I believed I would grow old with. We were just getting things paid off and looking forward to making plans for the rest of our lives.

Oh, the disbelief of losing him and God needing Bill just now, at this point in our lives. Disbelief can lead to sadness, sadness to loneliness, and right back to the beginning of the path of grief. This is a normal detour on the path. You will make leaps forward and then in one moment fall backward. It is frustrating. You'll ask yourself if you're crazy.

Grief, to me, sounds and feels like posttraumatic stress disorder (PTSD). I said that this is what I had to my doctor because this was how I was feeling every single day. Memories became the bomb explosions, and I felt like I had fight-or-flight behaviors. Once I fell asleep, I just wanted to stay there, forever. I didn't want to fight. I didn't want to go through another day of sadness, depression, or crying jags. I legitimately didn't want my new life (but I was not angry about it), and I really wanted to hit the life reset button to one week before his death—a bare minimum of time—just because my new life was an adjustment that I really, really didn't want to make. Reach out to those who truly understand what you're going through: Hope for Widows Foundation, www.hope4widows.org.

But my rational mind kept on telling me that this was just a step on the path of grief and that this too shall pass. It just takes time. Really? Seriously? How long is this time of which you speak? Days, months, years? I just wanted to die sometimes, to simply fall asleep and never wake up. I wanted to find a way to stop the sadness and disbelief somehow. I wondered why I was left behind here on earth. I wouldn't have done anything to myself. I'm against that from a spiritual aspect, and I wouldn't leave my daughter. I'm all that she has left. I know she has also felt the same way. She shared this with me a few months into our journey. This is also a normal thought that pops into your head as a new widow/widower, part of the grief process. If this becomes your only thought, please reach out to someone for help, National Suicide Prevention Lifeline (NSPL), 1-800-273-TALK (8255)

Death, as you already know, is permanent and not the solution to the current level of extreme sadness you are feeling.

I promise you this is just a point in time in the path of grief, and with the passage of time, you will see the beauty of life again. God is there with you, holding you, comforting you. Pray. Tell God how you feel! He is strong enough and cares enough to hear your words. He understands our loss and our feelings.

I just tried to keep on moving, keep on working, crying myself to sleep at night, taking on more and more at work to relieve myself of thinking about anything other than work. I had a wall up around me. I didn't want to talk to anyone, really. I wanted to only talk about work or dinner or something mundane enough to *not* send me into a torrent of tears and sadness.

But the problem was that I was having a terrible time getting out of bed on a daily basis. I was so emotionally and physically exhausted. First-year widows or widowers may have a tough time with regular life. Either you find a way to make it through, you fake it, or you just need to have a long break to take care of yourself. I know what I was feeling; your path may be different. Remember that you have entered the widow/widower zone where there are no hard-and-fast rules. You need to do what is right for you and no one else.

I have a coworker who ended up being a widow, without warning, just like me, in January 2018. She has gone through sickness, a heart attack, and a stroke, all in four months since her husband's passing. If no one understands that death and widowhood is a life sentence and can bring about other physical issues for the widow/widower, please read this and read this again.

I passed a kidney stone and my knee blew out after losing my husband. Death is stressful, unplanned, and permanent. Have empathy for the widow/widower—even if you don't know what to say. Work with the widow/widower even if you simply don't understand or practice empathy. Try not to give up on the widow/widower just because it prevents you from smooth planning of work or life.

I was doing the best I could when this happened. There's just not a quick timeframe to get through this—and he or she needs time to learn to breathe again.

Two Walls

DEATH BRINGS WITH IT TWO DIFFERENT WALLS. IF YOU SAY YOU ARE a widow/widower, be prepared for the first wall to come down and people to shy away from you. You start to feel like you have an infectious disease. No one wants to experience any part of your sadness. I do understand this part of humanity. People will do their best to change the subject as quickly as possible. Unfortunately, this is a normal reaction for many people. This action hurts the first few times it happens. But by month two, it will be normal, and you'll become used to this reaction. I wished for a different word to use for my situation. *Widow* is a harsh word for people. It's like saying "anthrax" to scare someone.

The second wall is one that you may create for yourself. Your wall of solitude—Superman's Fortress of Solitude. You may not want to deal with people, even close friends. Even though your friends want to help you, you may not even know how to tell them you need help. You don't know what you need or want. Widow fog. You may just simply be existing each day in order to go to sleep, blessed sleep.

Why are you downcast, O my soul? Why so disturbed within me? Put your hope in God, for I will yet praise him, my Savior and my God.

—Psalm 42:5

Emotional Pain and Sadness

EMOTIONAL PAIN, PHYSICAL PAIN, WITH THE ADDITION OF EXTREME sadness, this is a recipe for disaster all by itself; then you add in working your day job, and you can have an emotional meltdown. If you don't, then you are the strongest person I know, reader. My meltdown came when I couldn't get up in the morning no matter what time I went to bed; this was in July 2017. I could sleep for twelve hours straight and think nothing of it. This doesn't help when you need to be up, dressed, made-up, "caffeined up," and driving yourself to work in downtown St. Paul before 8:00 a.m., not to mention drive on one of the busiest freeways in Minnesota, park, and walk to work.

Just getting out of bed was an enormous chore. Getting a shower? A huge effort that was performed robotically, if it was done before work. Putting on makeup was something else altogether. I couldn't see the benefit or the need to do this unless I was going to see another person. It was all I could do to roll out of bed and turn on my computer and work on emails, contracts, and keep my meetings. I knew that my boss was not happy with me about working from home, but I just couldn't manage more than getting to bed, getting out of bed, and putting on my work persona.

Intuitively, I knew something more than just being a widow was going on in my life, but I had such widow fog and physical knee pain, I was just existing and utterly exhausted. I tried grief counseling, but I just could *not* stop crying during the time. Widow fog was real, and counseling interrupted my work life and didn't make my boss all that happy about an hour or so not working during the day.

Please help me. I am doing the absolute best that I can to get back to "normal." I just don't like or want my new normal. Chest feels tight, it's still hard to breathe.

> Oh, my anguish, my anguish! I writhe in pain. Oh, the agony of my heart! My heart pounds within me, I cannot keep silent. For I have heard the sound of the trumpet; I have heard the battle cry.
> —Jeremiah 4:19

15

Physical Pain

MY RIGHT KNEE BEGAN TO HURT ONCE I STARTED MY JOB DOWNTOWN in 2016. It was periodically painful, the osteoarthritis creeper disease that brings about the aching, burning, pain in one joint on either side of your body. There were days where simply getting up from a chair to walk to microwave my lunch was a study in unrelenting pain. The heating pad, by the end of the workday, was my new BFF, but it rarely gave me the relief I needed.

The death of my husband brought about stress that I can't even clearly articulate very well. I know that once the funeral was taken care of, and Brett and Kelley had left, my parents were still at the house, and I stayed in bed for thirty-six hours the next week passing a kidney stone. As if the emotional pain and sadness weren't enough, was a kidney stone a necessary requirement so soon after Bill died? I'm sure stress brought this on, as I was trying to bottle up my feelings to try to get through the business of his sudden death, and be a rock for others. I don't remember much during this time. I do know I was lying there in the bed that Bill and I shared, and I swear that I saw him lying there with me at one point. I'm sure I was in one of the moments between sleep and wakefulness. Was he really there? I want to believe he was, trying to comfort me in this first part of physical pain that would haunt my new life for the first year.

Once this was over, whew. My right knee was still painful; I just didn't take the time to gauge how much the pain was continuing to increase. I would limp occasionally, when the pain was intense. I was concentrating on adjusting to my new life and trying not to cry at inopportune moments. I buried myself in work and tried to do my best to pretend that I was doing good—as best I could, given my new shattered existence in this earthly life. I cried into my pillow, or on Frodo's fur, as quietly as I could night after night in the bed we once shared. I was still in the first two months of my new life as a widow. Deep anguish, sadness, and disbelief were still my BFFs. I cried for the times we would not have together, the love we shared, and for Kristen losing her dad. No words are adequate to explain my deep sadness. A scream or groan is the most appropriate articulation I could share.

I was still living in the bedroom, and I moved my desk to be in the same space. I was working from home once a week and trying to go into the office while still working through my sadness. I was really having a tough time getting out of bed, facing my coworkers (who were utterly amazing—thank you for your love and caring!), and simply trying to go back to my "old life." Everything brought Bill to the forefront of my mind. It was the hardest time of my life. I'm not sure I have the right words to explain what was going on in my head and my heart. I was so utterly lost, exhausted, in pain, emotionally drained, sad, deeply unhappy, and shoved into a new life I didn't want. Life without Bill was horrible. I just wanted to go to sleep and wake up to my old life with him.

I want you back! I need you! I need to be able to breathe again!

When Kristen moved in, this took away the room that my parents or guests used. My parents traveled from Florida to Minnesota for a biyearly big family reunion early in June of 2017. I was two months into my new life and wasn't sure if I could manage to go to the reunion. Every reunion, except the first one in 1983, included Bill as part of my life. I knew it would be difficult for me, but I knew I had to try. Because all of the rooms were full, I gave up my bedroom for my parents. I was not sleeping well in the bed we shared or even the room itself. I had to get out of the room. Having my parents there at that time gave me a plausible reason to simply give them the room.

I slept on the couch with Frodo (who is a bed hog, likes to sleep right up against you, and *hot*) and moved the desk out of the bedroom to allow for me to work. It was difficult to get used to, but I felt as if this was the right thing to do. I lived out of a clothes basket for a while. *But* my emotions would now be public knowledge; I held myself together, imagining that I was inside a superglue bottle. I was tense beyond measure, and it was all of my own making. My right knee was super painful. I was really beginning to noticeably limp. I was really trying to keep a grip on myself, get through the day, and hold my emotions in as best I could. I wanted to be strong and just continue to move forward. I was a perfectly put-together chaotic disaster.

I just miss you, Bill.

> Turn to me and be gracious to me, for I am lonely and afflicted. The troubles of my heart have multiplied; free me from my anguish. Look upon my affliction and my distress and take away all my sins.
> —Psalm 25:16—18

C. B. SCHNEIDER

Month 3

THE LONELINESS AT NIGHT IS A HUGE, GAPING BLACK HOLE. I REALIZED my current house came with a larger yard that I really didn't want to care for now. I wanted to move out of the house we had shared for twenty years because of the yard and the driveway for winter. This was my excuse to everyone. Really, I just couldn't find a space in the house where there wasn't a memory of Bill or us as a family.

It was June 2017, extremely hot and humid. On June 11, Lino Lakes, Minnesota (and surrounding communities), got hit by a freak storm that left houses and streets damaged and looking like a war zone. My house and two cars were damaged by hail. I admit this new "fun" stopped me from looking at moving to deal with home repair and dealing with insurance again. Seriously? I wondered why I needed one more thing to work through. I was already knee-deep (no pun intended!) in trying to get a handle on all the monthly bills, remove Bill's name, and try to understand how I was going to make it through without his paycheck, and trying to work. My right knee was also super painful. I was depressed, sad, bottled-up, on edge, and exhausted. Sleep, blessed sleep, was my best friend.

Remember I wrote to call your local utility company first? Dealing with home and auto insurance had me calling their 1-800 number a total of ten times to try to get them to remove my spouse's name, fix the email address, change the phone number from his to mine, and then, they forgot to make the change in their own system to allow for this. Checks were printed out in both names for the house and car damages a few times. I felt as if I were talking to a wall, having to figure out all of the issues for each company. I don't plan to name the company that I was dealing with. I would rather make this suggestion/comment for all service companies.

- People die every single day.
- I am not the only widow/widower calling your company to ask for help. *Help me!*
- I have enough life stuff to deal with now, and a little bit of help from you can go a long way toward making this easier for me.
- I need you to do what you say you will do, no matter what.

I think a few minutes in a widow's shoes would teach every company a thing or two about what it is like to lose someone. It's not my job to understand what you say about your company's inner workings, and I should *not* have to try. I reserve the right to be a *dumb customer,* and it is *your* job to solve the account challenges you may have in your computer system.

Ever heard of lean or continuous improvement? Lean out or improve your back end to make your process easier for customers. Being a widow means fighting against a world that doesn't help widows remove their deceased spouse from the monthly invoices without a fight or having to set up a new account and stop your current services to accomplish a company's needs in the computer systems. I can't even tell you how many times I heard, "I'm sorry for your loss. How can I help you?" I wish I would have kept count. The first time you hear this, you will believe they care, and you will cry all over again.

Tell me what you need (company) in order to help me (the widow/widower), and then you (company) need to follow through to fix my account on your side. Please understand that you may need to repeat yourself. I have widow fog, and it's real.

The Necessary Items

Final Death Certificate

YOU WILL NEED TO MAKE SURE YOU HAVE ENOUGH COPIES OF THE final death certificate on hand; you will also need to scan one in and save it on your computer or your phone. Some companies will require that you send an original to them—understand—sending a fax is the same as the original document and constitutes a legal document in a court of law, and you should be able to send the final death certificate through the fax as often as you need to. I was also able to email a picture via my iPhone to one company. Not all of the companies you may need to deal with have their back-end process together, so you will need to confirm *exactly* what each company requires. I suggest taking notes about each call you make that include the following:

- date
- time
- person's name

- what you said
- what the other person said to you

You may need this when you have to call again, or again after your second, third, or fourth call. This is so ridiculous, and this will zap your energy. However, use any anger you may have inside and fight to make sure that people hear you, new widow! I broke down a few times—both on the phone and off. Why would I think to call up any service company to tell you my husband died? I don't get a thrill out of doing something like this. It makes me relive losing him over and over. Can you hear the message I am saying? Is there anything more I can write to make this crystal clear?

Help widows and widowers. We are doing the best we can in every aspect of our newly shattered lives. Empathy and follow-through on your side would go a long way to help us out of the mess we didn't ask to be in the middle of—ever!

We live in a digital age, where we can pay for things with our phones. We have way too many passwords, and we don't share this information with anyone. Our jobs tell us this every day, making it an offense close to unethical behavior, potential for being fired. Think of the digital age in two different ways. You have your work life and your personal life. In the case of your personal life, share your passwords for your digital payments in this digital age and the password for your phone. Your surviving spouse will thank you.

Obituary Notice

USE YOUR CELL PHONE TO TAKE A PICTURE OF THE OBITUARY NOTICE
that appeared in the selected (paper) newspaper, or you can take
a picture of the online obituary or favorite the link. There are
certain companies you can contact that may accept this notice as
the official notice of death. I used this to shut down my husband's
LinkedIn account, which worked perfectly.

Shutting Down a Digital Life

BILL TOOK CARE OF ALL THE PAYMENTS FOR OUR HOUSEHOLD SINCE we were married. In the last few years, he set up auto-payments for the majority of our monthly bills. We never thought for a moment that death would separate us in 2017. Neither of us shared our passwords for our phones either. Based on whether you have Apple or Android, you may end up with a problem trying to unlock the phone. Apple refused to unlock a phone for the government. They won't unlock a phone for a widow/ widower either. I believe in what Apple decided, and I support them for this decision 100 percent.

You will need to figure out if you can share your phone password. I have always used my personal phone for my work life; I never wanted to carry two phones. While whatever corporate entity insisted that no one knows your phone password, I wholeheartedly believe that you should be able to trust your spouse (or someone!) enough to have your phone password, regardless if you use your personal phone for work. I know deep in my heart that I trusted my husband with everything in this life. I could have trusted him with my iPhone password. Fire me if this is wrong in this digital world! How can any company hurt me any worse than losing the love of my life?

This digital world we live in means we must have one person with whom we can share our passwords—from phones to digital accounts. More than one person should have the key to a lockbox and knows where to look should a terrible event happen. This is the reality that I faced; no passwords were written down or shared with me. Yes, Bill's phone was locked, and I didn't know the four-digit password. He also had a password app on his iPhone. If I had known either password(s), the first three months of my new life might have been a bit easier to work through. (I may not have made a few late payments on my car loan!) We were good corporate citizens, and this truly didn't help me when it came to his iPhone. I now have a phone that can't be used; it sits in a drawer because I can't fix it. Lesson learned. But what a waste of an iPhone.

Shutting down a digital life is not easy at all. I did use the online obituary as an attachment to an email to start a conversation about his death for my cell phone provider. I even sent it to my home/car insurance agent too. All my insurance agent did was to update that he died—nothing else was done. It still took twenty-one phone calls to customer service to try to get them to fix their back-office issues. By the way, if you become the only driver on your car-insurance policy, your rates may be raised with some companies. You may need to shop around for car insurance. Find a company that does not care that you are no longer married, as if it were your choice in the matter. You are now "unmarried" but still have the same number of cars and a house. There are not many reasons, other than timing of the policy renewal itself, why the rates should rise at all when this happens, but it can happen.

Once you have the final death certificate, you are now ready to begin some of the most difficult work from your loss. Calling companies, removing your spouse's name, and moving all things into your name can be a huge chore that saps your energy, your fighting spirit, and leaves you drained. I felt as if I was the only widow in the world fighting for what was right and just. I am not the only widow on the planet, but it appears that not all companies are not adept at helping. The script only includes, "I'm so sorry for your loss." The part where they ask how they can help ... this is the difficult part.

Actual Death Benefit

BILL HAD AN INSURANCE POLICY THAT I WAS NOT AWARE OF HIS NEW job; I was aided by the HR person and pointed in the right direction immediately. With the provision of the final death certificate, Bill's insurance benefit from his job paid out automatically. I used this death benefit to pay off his car loan, thus ridding myself of one automatic monthly payment. Subsequently, I had to go to the DMV to remove his name from the title itself.

The death benefit that I had through my job for Bill was very slow to react. However, by law, insurance companies must pay out a minimal amount to the beneficiary. One check received initially does *not* mean that you have accepted a partial payment as "payment in full." Note: you may not receive the full amount right away. Insurance companies must perform their own due diligence before providing full payout. It took six months, numerous calls and notes, and starts and stops for final payout to be provided. I suppose there are a few reasons for this that are specific to Bill, or not. One, he was generally quite healthy, hardly ever sick; two, and in two years, had only three doctor visits. He did have high blood pressure and was on medication to provide control. Little did we know that he had heart disease that was the main contributor to his death from a massive heart attack.

Working through this task was horrendous. You may be dealing with a third-party record provider for health records. You have to sign off that you are able to put in the request for the records, hope that the records make it to the right department for the benefit. I suggest asking for the records yourself. Not that this will help you; unfortunately, even if you send it to the insurance company, any mistake made by the third-party provider for the total number of records will end up creating a delay. Even when the insurance company has the records, they have a window of time for review of the records. Either this will be sufficient, or they will create a new delay for you.

For me, the insurance company then had to review whether there was a waiting period for benefit payouts. Then, they have to look at the policy itself for any "outs" that would allow them not to pay the full benefit to you. Note: the ultimate payout may be larger due to the interest the value of the death benefit is incurring as it is sitting and not being paid out to you. There is *no* tax on death benefit payouts for the amount; however, there is tax on the interest that such value accrues.

Some companies may have a twelve-month time frame in which you must have the policy in place prior to any payout made to the beneficiary. In my case, I was fortunate that there wasn't a waiting period. Six months of fighting for the payout was incredibly painful. Even when I finally received the second and final payout, I burst into tears. I still would have rather had this life with Bill in it. While the money is helpful and provides a level of relief, it's still tough to cash the check when you now it "represents" the person you love. This is where you will need to think with your head rather than your heart. Cry first—then deposit the check.

I created a very *simple* budget that you can download from my website: www.digitalagewidow.com. I needed to know what was going out and coming in, as well as how paying things off would impact the overall value left from the death benefit. This was not something I had to deal with, so it was new to me. You may have something more complex already in use; if so, disregard.

I suggest your first widow/widower call be to your local utility company. I called the City of Lino Lakes to remove my husband's name and put mine into the first spot for our water bill. This was the easiest call I made regarding my husband's death, and I wish it would have been the first one I did. I made calls based on when the payments were due and what I could see was being paid out of our checking account. This was my attempt to work through breathing better.

Calling your electricity provider should also be done. This also was not that difficult—only one call took care of the name change. These two calls didn't require a death certificate as proof. It's some of the other calls that created so much pain—insurance, car, house, and death benefit—that were the prizefights.

Bank Accounts

IT MAY BE A GOOD THING TO CLOSE YOUR SPOUSE'S DEBIT CARD; however, if your payments are tied to this card, you will need to make changes to the online accounts before you close the card. You can leave your spouse's name on the bank account if you believe that you will be getting checks made out to your spouse. However, you will be able to cash checks under your spouse's name if you bring a death certificate to the bank. They will make a copy of the certificate and keep it on file for the account. This is your call; however, with fraud on the rise in this digital age, once your spouse is added to the deceased list from the Social Security Administration, it might be in your best interest to remove your spouse's name from all bank accounts as soon as possible. You just never know what fraudsters are up to.

Social Security

THE FUNERAL DIRECTOR WILL REPORT YOUR SPOUSE'S DEATH TO THE Social Security Administration; however, it might be in your best interest to check out this URL as well: https://www.ssa.gov/pubs/EN-05-10008.pdf. I reported his death to the SSA via a phone call; I may have been the first or second person to call about my husband's death. I then had to schedule a one-hour phone call to go over what benefits I could receive both now and in the future. You need to be aware that you will receive a death benefit check from the SSA. The current value is $255.00 and takes a few months for you to receive it. Woo-hoo, party.

Cell Phone

T-MOBILE WAS THE CELL PHONE CARRIER BILL AND I SELECTED around 2002 or thereabouts. I checked the website FAQs first to find out the best way to start to make changes to the account. Please know that I didn't originally know the password for our account; I had to guess. I ended up with the correct four-digit password for the account. (This must be one of the few miracles I encountered in my initial journey as a widow and accounts in general.) I had to shut down my father-in-law's cell phone (due to dementia) as well as my husband's phone number. Note: don't turn off your spouse's phone until you can unlock it. I added both my parents to the account, which was now under my name. I was able to accomplish this with the help of a very nice young woman who helped go through all the hoops needed in T-Mobile's back office to obtain the old agreement that I had that allowed for up to five phones at a low cost.

I will be a loyal T-Mobile customer; this is one carrier that does help its customers (widows), and I didn't have to make a ton of calls to fix my issues. T-Mobile gets my highest rating for helping customers, both via the customer service center and the local store locations. Shout out to the Blaine, Minnesota, T-Mobile location for being a great place for helping widows and my nondigital parents who are learning to be techie.

24

Car Loans

IF YOUR CAR(S) ARE IN BOTH NAMES, YOU CAN PAY OFF YOUR CAR loan(s) with your death benefit. However, you will need to change the title at your local DMV. You will need to bring the title, death certificate, and your insurance information. This will take between four to eight weeks for you to receive a new title in your name. If you donate your car, the only way you can claim the donation for tax purposes is to donate to a reputable organization who provides you with all of the documentation you need for taxes. I donated our spare car to the veterans.

25

Student Loans

I PAID OFF ALL STUDENT LOANS WITH PART OF THE DEATH BENEFIT received. I needed to get rid of as many payments as I could to determine where I stood financially as a widow without two incomes. Truthfully, I was relieved to be able to do this for me and our daughter. Erasing debt feels good. Each widow/ widower's situation may be different; you need to do what you believe to be in your best interest no matter what anyone says to you. There are no rules you need to follow; instead, follow your heart (and your brain) to determine the path that is best for you. I followed biblical truths I know regarding debt payment.

Selling the Elm Street House

I HAD TO SELL THE HOUSE; THERE WERE TOO MANY MEMORIES OF Bill and our life together. I know that the social norm is to "not make big decisions until after the first year." I had been wanting to move for years, but Bill thought it would be prudent to stay. I truly felt that I would not be able to move forward with my life if I stayed in the same house. There are some widows/widowers who really want to stay in the same house, comforted by their memories, and only you can determine what is going to be best for you. Don't let a societal norm make decisions for you or your need to move forward in your new life.

I felt stifled, my chest was heavy, and I was way too tense, living in the house on Elm Street; I really don't know why. I just knew selling it would be the best thing for me. I thought about the love that could continue to be in the house, the large yard enjoyed by kids, with the proximity of schools being a great selling point. I contacted my old next-door neighbor and asked her to sell my house.

After a few cosmetic touch-ups (thanks, family!) and many

boxes packed up, the house was ready for pictures, and then for the first open house. Before the first scheduled open house a request came in to see the house already. Lo and behold, the car that pulled in my driveway ended up being a coworker from a past job. The God part about this, I had teased my girlfriend about buying my house—here she was, with her husband, to see my house. Since their realtor was late, I took them on a tour of the house. I pointed out all of the differentiating factors of the house that I thought made it unique and different from the other cookie-cutter houses on the block. They loved the story of the wall outside the downstairs bedroom. I cried, reliving the love of the painted wall scribbling for them. My first real deep breath!

This young couple put in a bid on my house at the listed price the same night they saw it. I was so happy to sell the Elm Street house to a young couple (people I already knew!) with kids, who would take on the story of the wall and create their own story in a house that was filled with love. This was totally God inspired and directed, and I understood my need for selling. God was providing them with the house they prayed for; He was also providing me with a lovely young couple who would love the house as much as Bill and I had. I felt joyous with the determination of selling our beloved house.

27

Other Phone Calls

FAMILY PHONE CALLS CAN CREATE ADDITIONAL MOMENTS OF SADNESS for everyone, especially the new widow. The concern that comes through the phone line can be overwhelming, and I know I cried each time I talked to a family member, such as a close aunt. Sometimes it's hard to hide the absolute breakdown you have on the phone; but, I promise, these calls do get easier with elapsed time. At seven months, I can hold back my breakdown until I hang up, and then it's a shorter breakdown.

I speak out loud to Bill how much I miss him, and then I get busy with something that needs to be done. I allow the pain, the sadness, and the tears their moment. Getting the sadness out allows me to be able to move forward, and each time I allow this, the time period becomes shorter and shorter for the breakdown.

Don't think for a moment that just because the sadness is shorter that the pain is easier. It still rips your heart into pieces, can make you sick to your stomach, or make you feel like going back to bed to hide and wallow in your sadness. How *you* experience grief will be different from what is written herein. The goal is to share the experience so that you know that you are *not* crazy— right now.

Solitude

As a new widow/widower, being with people only enhances your sadness for your missing spouse. People, places, and relationships shift slightly. There might be awkwardness on the part of friends, even family. Your coworkers may not know what to say to you from one day to the next, even family and friends. Let them know you need time alone to process your grief.

I needed months of solitude, interspersed with doses of people. One of the challenges that I had at the same time I was deep in grief was the intense pain in my right knee. Not only did I have widow fog, I had pain fog, sadness fog, feeling-lost fog. I recently bought a candle to burn named "Sand and Fog." This is my dry humor at acknowledging my "fog" and adding in sand to try to ground myself.

You can't judge yourself during the first year of your grief. My mantra since becoming a widow:

This is my path, and there's no right or wrong; no societal norms/ rules will be applied. With prayer, I will move forward as God directs.

It took me months to truly learn that this is the best way for me to deal with my grief. Note that you *should* be able to "have emotions" when *you* need to—no matter where you are, what you are doing, and who you are with. If the people around you don't understand this, or they are uncomfortable with either you or your loss, then you need to rethink your situation. If this is your work environment, you may need to take a break from working, either using the Family Medical Leave Act (FMLA) or short-term or long-term disability. Use this if you have it and you believe you need it and your doctor agrees with you. You have to take care of yourself from an emotional or physical standpoint. No one can truly understand the utter devastation the loss of a spouse unless they have walked in your shoes, or belong to the widows club.

Even if a friend belongs to the widows/widowers club, note that each relationship (thus each loss) is similar, but still different. The loss of my husband feels like the loss of my arm or leg; my other half is missing, and it can be so lonely. My husband was my best friend, my better half, my world. I feel like I have lost my twin in this world. I often felt alone, lonely, bereft, out of sorts, and I wonder what my purpose is in this new life. I'm glad to make it through one day at a time, and I need to keep myself centered on God in order to move forward.

Without my faith, I honestly don't know how I could even get through each day. I did try to journal, but I quickly ran out of time every day with sadness, work, family, friends, and general life. I was also in so much physical pain that I could not clearly articulate my utter sadness, and I needed solitude. When I did think about it, it was bedtime, and that's when I would need to breakdown and cry myself to sleep. I chose this method for months, and I admit, it was all I could do.

I just miss you, Bill! I am trying so hard to move out of sadness for me and joy for you.

My prayer: God, please help me through my sadness and help me to find the blessing you have provided to me even in the midst of this trial.

Past and Present Pain

THE EMOTIONAL PAIN YOU FEEL FROM YOUR LOSS ONLY HEIGHTENS any type of physical pain you may have been experiencing prior to becoming a widow. I started a new job in March of 2016; I worked in downtown St. Paul, Minnesota. This means you have to pay to park somewhere and walk to your office building. While this is a good thing for exercise, what I didn't realize was that my right knee was bone on bone on the inside of my knee. The kneecap itself was fine; it was the bones on the inside of the right knee that had a corporate meeting minute after minute, hour after hour, and day after day that had me in such extreme pain. Plus, the cartilage had calcified and was breaking up inside my knee. The pain increased slowly, but by the time of Bill's death, it had become moderately painful. By July of 2017, my knee had become so painful and white-hot that it was impacting my emotional stability. Not only was my sadness taking over, I was depressed. The complete tangle of depression.

Even though depression does not run in my family, I had been diagnosed with depression in 2000. I felt the light switch turn off, and I went to the doctor to get some help. In the same year, I had to have surgery for my jaws; the pain of the upper and lower jaws growing together (like stalactites and stalagmites in a cave) was also incredibly intense. Surgery repaired my TMJ joints by creating a new disc with skin from my abdomen to be placed inside the jaw joint itself. This was a ten-hour surgery that provided immediate relief from pain that had steadily increased over time. When I woke up from the surgery, my epiphany was intense. The jaw pain was gone. I didn't even realize how incredible the pain was for me until it disappeared from my life.

This has been how my life has been since 1982, when I was hit by a drunk driver. Even though my life with Bill started in 1986, I believe it is important to outline the level of pain tolerance that I have experienced in my life. I can tolerate pain increasing over time; however, there comes a time when the pain is too much and the impact it has on your emotional health has to be taken care of, period.

The crash happened on December 23, 1982, while I was driving on childhood streets where I learned to drive. The other car turned left when the light turned yellow, and I was in the middle of an intersection. I was traveling at thirty miles per hour, the official speed of the street itself, and the impact propelled me up into the windshield, hitting my head and breaking it into a "V" shape. As I came down with the motion of the car, I slammed my jaw on the dashboard, hitting the front of my neck and body on the steering wheel. My left knee slammed into the bottom of the dashboard, and I felt like a bus had hit me in each individual part of my body.

Little did I know that this crash would impact me for the rest of my life. Even though this was a horrific event for an eighteen-year-old, which sidelined my young life, I would not change a single thing about this event. This event was a pivotal moment in my young life; it eventually brought me to my husband, which in turn brought me to have my daughter, which brought me to this point in my life. There is always a plan that God has for your life. He turns tragedy into good things!

> For I know the plans I have for you, declares the Lord, plans for welfare and not for evil, to give you future and a hope.
> —Jeremiah 29:11

I have lived by the following verse for all of my life since my confirmation in middle school (junior high to us Baby Boomers.)

> God grant me the serenity to accept the things I cannot change, courage to change the things I can, and wisdom to know the difference.
> —Reinhold Niebuhr (1892-1971)

Granted, everyone gets ticked off and wonders, "Why me?" at certain points throughout their lives. I am no different than anyone else, but faith remains my cornerstone for everything that happens in this physical life. The impact of the 1982 crash created the following changes in my life—most, before meeting Bill—and many because of the initial crash and injuries I faced—which continue to impact me to this day. Bill knew about all of this and still chose to make me his life partner. I just thought we would have forever.

1. Head injury. Brain bruise on the right side of my brain. It increases and decreases, and I have no idea of the final impact. I can have headaches that are debilitating and sharp pains that can happen for no reason. I choose to live my life no matter what.

C. B. SCHNEIDER

2. Loss of Long-Term Memory. I have memories that come back like a slow-motion film inside my head. I remembered Abraham Lincoln learning by candlelight, and he ended up being one of the greatest presidents in our history, in my humble opinion. If he could do this, then I could relearn what I didn't remember, once I figured out what I didn't remember. This is a cyclical issue and one that continues even today. This also appears to have created a faster circuit for "seeing" what needs to be done for projects or the answers to questions. Blessing and curse all at the same time. I have learned to work through this and enjoy helping people.

3. Thyroid. My brain shut off my thyroid, creating Hashimoto's disease, allergies, celiac disease, and eventually a hysterectomy and other fun endocrinology things.

4. TMJ surgeries to replace the shattered jaw discs, 1983, 1984, 1985, 1992, 2000. Plus, a cyst on the left side of my face, below my upper jawbone, that made me ill, 2015.

5. Teeth challenges for my original beautiful thirty-two-tooth smile. I think I have far fewer now—maybe 15 or so? I would have to look and count to be sure.

6. 2008 sleep apnea. My brain stops breathing, so my CPAP machine is crucial every night. I've been the proud owner of a machine since 2008. Bill used to call me Darth Vader at night, but he did love the cool air I ended up blowing at him like a fan in his face. He loved sleeping with a fan at night—a real fan—plus me. Now I just end up blowing air at Frodo.

7. Back problems. My head was crooked on my spine for thirty-two years. I worked with an atlas chiropractor, who adjusted my atlas bone. (Thank you, Hejny Chiropractic!) My right leg was shorter than my left because of the atlas bone; the pain had become *so* intense over time for my

entire back. Some days were *so* incredibly bad! Pain is an unrelenting companion.

8. Family arthritis. Arthritis found me at twenty-two years old. Left elbow, both knees, thumbs, and lower back were the areas that hurt the most. Thumbs stopped hurting once they were deformed; I had originally hoped that the rest of the body would be the same.

With the loss of Bill, the depression medicine that I had been on for seventeen years appeared to have failed. I was an emotional disaster by month four; I felt the depression switch turn on once again. I really didn't care about much more than my family, friends, Frodo, and work. Taking care of my loyal companion became my reason for living. I was a solitary recluse for months five and six. I could not see the joy in life, could not find the importance of doing my job, and just wanted to sleep because of my fatigue and pain from my right knee. I was having trouble getting out of bed because I was so tired. I didn't want to eat. I relied on my family and a few friends heavily to sense-check myself to see if I had lost my mind at times. It became abundantly clear to me that I needed to figure out what was going on with me, other than being a sad, lonely widow.

I made an appointment with my doctor to talk about my fatigue, my lack of emotional control, and the pain in my knee. By the end of widow month six, my doctor had written me out of work. On September 25, 2017, the first day of my short-term disability, was also our thirtieth wedding anniversary. I made dinner, lit our wedding candle, and ate dinner with Bill's picture instead of him.

Oh, I miss you so much! I thought we had forever.

Month Seven

I SPENT MONTH SEVEN SLEEPING FOR MOST OF THE DAY WHILE MY right knee became progressively worse. I was not 100 percent sure that my meds were the problem; I thought it was just my sadness of losing Bill and the fact that I had gone back to work too soon upon his death and the physical pain. Honestly, I just couldn't function; I couldn't concentrate, read, or think straight, so I had a difficult time figuring out what I wanted to do versus what I should do. All I could do was my best to take care of myself and Frodo. I ended up letting the housework go and just watched TV because I couldn't do much else. I could not think or concentrate through the pain. Walking in the house was painful, stairs were terrifying, and going somewhere became a nightmare.

I set up a doctor appointment to have an X-ray to understand what was going on with my right leg. The X-ray clearly showed bone on bone. There's a process for this that must be followed when you are too young for a replacement surgery. Once I had the shot of cortisone in my right knee, it worked for fifteen days. I was pain-free, and I realized just how bad my knee was, with the pain increasing daily since Bill's death and moving to a new house. I ended up having a series of three injections of glucosamine; this was the next step in the medical-and-insurance process, along with a walking cane and a handicapped hangtag for my car. I would love to say that this was the process that alleviated the pain, but it wasn't. Too young to live a life of not working daily—this is no way to live. I was too exhausted to go through this level of pain and not be able to do something as simple as dust, vacuum, or just simply walk, let alone think or concentrate. The only way to alleviate the pain was to sleep. Good thing that I was able to sleep. Intense pain creates exhaustion. Oh, the blessed escape that sleep can be.

My dad went through the same exact thing with his right knee. Osteoarthritis is a painful disease, and there's no way I am going to live like I am twenty to thirty years older than I am. I need to be able to move on with my life—through the pain and the adjustment of being alone and no longer part of a unit or a complete whole.

I pushed for the medicine change in month seven. It would take a month, and I would need to be monitored on a weekly basis to ensure that the change was effective. You must increase one and decrease the other. This was one of the best ideas and decisions I made, but it would take time and patience to make the switch.

One of the best outcomes I found from the med switch was the ability to dream and then the ability to remember my dreams. I know that I used to dream and remember my dreams when Bill was alive, and then after his death, nothing. Dreams felt like a huge black hole for me. Taking a new medicine brought back my dreams and memories, and gave me some of the energy that I was missing by removing part of the fatigue, which allowed me to get out of bed when I had to. New lease on life! Well, sort of. I was able to breathe—not deeply yet—*no rules, no judgment.*

Month Eight

I STRUGGLED TO GO BACK TO MY JOB AFTER SHORT-TERM DISABILITY (round one). All I can think is that this was where I was working when Bill was alive, when he died, and the emotional reality of missing him daily. I was not sure how I could go back without breaking down and feeling like my life had just simply stopped at the point of his death. I just didn't know if I can do this.

Another thought was walking on the icy/snowy downtown sidewalks with a cane and an unreliable right knee. I was hoping that going back to work would allow me to feel more "normal." But what is the definition of normal when it comes to being a widow or widower? Lost, alone, no longer part of a marriage unit, sad? What does normal feel like? I got nothing. And why is there no other word to describe my new life other than the word *widow*? I feel I need to make up a new word that doesn't create a wall between people when describing who I am at this point in my life. Another designation is "unmarried," but this is also not correct. The only reason I am unmarried is due to death, thus still labeling me as a widow.

It's a vicious cycle back to a label for the rest of the world to define my status.

Since Bill's death, I needed to make changes in my life for *me* to move forward. This was a new experience, thinking about me, instead of *us*. I sold our house, made some changes to refresh my appearance, paid off the debts for both Kristen and me, becoming part of the financial-clean-slate club. Still a card-holding member of the digital-age widow's club, with debts gone and a new house (to make new memories), while still holding onto the best memories of my life with Bill.

Oh, how I miss your voice, your touch, and your comfort. Your love.

Don't get me wrong. All the changes that I have made may not be right for you in your journey. You need to do what helps *you* cope and exist in your new life. If you need to keep your spouse's clothes—then keep them! If you need to stay in the house where you made your memories—then stay there! There are *no* rules that you should be following now no matter what anyone tells you or tries to tell you. Only *you* can decide what makes sense for you right now.

Even when well-meaning people try to caution you about making major changes the first year, you need to do what is right for your journey; sometimes the change can be God inspired and may have nothing to do with you directly. While I understand this on the surface, death created an instant change in life that forced me into my new life as a widow. Change can be a positive thing. You have look for the blessing in the changes, no matter how hard it is or how crazy this sounds.

I know that there are reasons for Bill's death that I am not able to understand right now. I have faith that someday I will understand. For now, my heart rejoices that he is with the Lord and I continue to pray for comfort and direction in this life, despite my sadness of not being with him.

C. B. SCHNEIDER

Oh Lord, please help me to go through the sadness to get to the joy.
Help me to breathe deeply again.

> Do not let your hearts be troubled. Trust in God.
> —John 14:1

I made it to the office throughout January, walking carefully with my cane. I did trip and fall a few times, but there wasn't a whole lot I could do about it. By the time I reached my cube, my knee was throbbing and complaining. Walking to the bathroom or going to heat up my lunch was a study in trying to keep my face from showing the pain. I'm sure I was not successful. By the time I made it home, let Frodo out and fed him, and made my dinner, I was done each day. Tears didn't happen every night anymore because of sadness; sometimes it was just the pain leaking out on my face.

To add to this, there was a heavy snowfall in early February. I was already going to be late for work because of the snow, and I was worried since I was just barely back at work. I forgot about all of the snow that gets piled up at the end of the driveway after the snowplow goes through. Yes, *that* snow. The snow that had always been magically gone before I left. The snow that my beloved husband had cleared out before I was awake. His early morning rising meant taking care of business for his princesses.

My anxiety was already a *ten* because of the snow. I backed out of the garage and got stuck in the snow. I called Kristen to get up, get dressed, and help me get unstuck. I put the car in reverse and then shoved into drive in my attempt to get unstuck. Kristen was pushing when I was reversing. No luck, I was stuck on the new snow pile at the end of the driveway. How stupid I was at that moment, anxiety brought tears, frustration brought sadness. Kristen ran into the garage, grabbed a carpet piece, cut it in half, and stuck the carpet under each front tire. I reversed and voila! I was now able to drive to work.

Later on in the day, it fully dawned on me how the driveway was always taken care of: Bill. At first, I was sad that I hadn't thought that through. Then I realized that this was a first-year-snowfall widow moment. I knew then I would end up having many such moments for a few years. I held back a second wave of tears until bedtime. Oh, for the end of that day! Blessed sleep to escape my physical and emotional pain!

Oh, Bill! I miss you so much it hurts! (Literally!)

Don't wait until your beloved is gone from this Earth to realize all of the good things that he or she does for you. Thank each other daily for the small acts of love.

Months Nine and Ten

In early February, I came down with a virus. I asked to work from home rather than share my contagion. While I was standing still, making myself lunch, I heard a "pop" in my right knee. I hit the floor. I must have sat on the floor trying to figure out how to get up for fifteen minutes. The tears were flowing freely, the pain was white-hot, and I was terrified about what had just happened to my knee. I finally managed to get up, skipped lunch, and hobbled back to my laptop to keep on working after swallowing a few aspirins.

At the end of that day, when Kristen came home, I told her what had happened. She took me to the doctor the next morning because I couldn't put much pressure on my knee. I bumped down the stairs on my butt to get to the garage, where I screamed out in pain after limping to her car, where I screamed again as I moved my right leg into the car itself. I thought about Bill, my loss, the physical pain, and all the reasons why I was in this current mess. I just sat there, trying to keep my emotions in check. No one wants to deal with an emotional train wreck (widow) all the time.

Standing for the X-ray was excruciating. My knee looked the same as the last X-ray, so it was determined that the meniscus must have ripped. My doc wrote me off work for a week to take pain pills. I could hardly walk, so driving was out the question, as was logical, cognitive thought. I emailed my boss about being off for a week; he suggested short-term disability until my upcoming surgery.

I know this was not expected, completely unplanned, and a total pain in the butt for my boss. I hit the worried button about my job. FMLA had run out, and I thought, *What a perfect time to replace me.* It hadn't even been a year since my husband had passed. My life was messy, I was a widow (like others before and after me), but I was doing the best I could, given my new life. I knew that this was the next thing to happen to me in my journey. No one had to tell me. I just intuitively knew this was the next big thing.

I didn't choose to be a widow, I didn't choose to have a bad knee, and I didn't choose to have to replace my meds. I know. I know. Life is not fair. It just felt like this would be way too much for this widow to lose a job as well. It feels like being thrown away—all because something unplanned totally disrupted my previously smooth and "planned" life where I was married and I had help.

Until you have to face tragedy in this life, you can't understand the path someone is on. I wish nothing but the best in life for all involved. Some things are just simply beyond a person's control. New "normal" courtesy of widowhood.

> Do not be anxious about anything, but in everything, by prayer and petition, with thanksgiving, present your requests to God. And the peace of God, which transcends all understanding, will guard your hearts and your minds in Christ Jesus."
>
> —Philippians 4:6–7

I ended up on short-term disability for the second time in less than a year, until my scheduled knee-replacement surgery on February 28, 2018. I was informed that I would be replaced in my job; the posting would go up soon. The original posting for the job had taken six months to fill; I assumed that it would take at least a few months to fill the job. I felt as if I had been kicked to the curb because of becoming a widow with a bum knee. It's just another part of the journey, but it still hurt my soul. Perhaps this was just another part of this new chapter; either way, I would accept the hand that I had been dealt with professionalism, humility, and a servant attitude.

> What then, shall we say in response to this? If God is
> for us, who can be against us?
> —Romans 8:31

Month Eleven

THE SURGERY WENT WELL. THE DOCTOR WAS AMAZED I HAD walked that long, based on the carnage he found when he opened my knee. I had the bone-on-bone issue, which was known, so a partial replacement fixed this. What no one had known until that moment was that the cartilage had calcified and was breaking up inside my knee. It was like a pothole inside my knee, and there was a minor tear in the meniscus as well. No wonder!! I had a moment of realization when I was told this information. Not only had I been honest about the pain, I had experienced a few good days with my knee, but more painful days where just being awake felt like more than I could handle. Physical pain ties into the emotional pain, making both forefront in your life and your thoughts. A recipe for sadness and pain.

Surgical pain could be handled; now it was about healing and working through my emotions since I was more fully aware and using my brain. The pain fog was beginning to lift. My heart was a bit lighter. It was easier to laugh about funny or stupid things.

I was still lonely; nothing could erase this pain. I continued to pray for healing—both physical and emotional.

I still miss you, Bill. I now understand that I always will. I just need to find the strength to stop the water leakage on my face. God, please help me!

> Brothers, I do not consider myself yet to have taken hold of it. But one thing I do: Forgetting what is behind and straining toward what is ahead. I press on toward the goal to win the prize for which God has called me heavenward in Christ Jesus.
>
> —Philippians 3:13–14

Month Twelve

PHYSICAL THERAPY WAS MY WORLD. NOW THAT I WOULD HAVE A functional knee, I thought I could tackle everything. I threw myself into managing the swelling and physical therapy. I was still going down the stairs like a five-year-old, but I was getting stronger physically and surer of my new knee's abilities. The physical pain was much improved. I was able to concentrate for longer periods of time. I was finally able to read a book without wondering about what I'd just read. I felt this was a small victory for me.

However, sitting upright on a chair, even for a half hour, made my leg swell. I was concerned that despite the progress I had made, I would not be able to sit at a desk and work for eight hours. My position was filled in late April. I now didn't have a job, but I was still an employee of the company. My perception was that I would not be accommodated for light duty or working from home because I no longer had the same job. I tried not to worry about this fact. I was still working through my loss and figuring out what I could or couldn't yet do with my new knee.

In April, we had a snowstorm that dumped a total of eighteen inches of snow, and no one was around to help me clear the driveway. I started to shovel, thinking this would be better than trying to run the snowblower. I fell a few times and ended up exhausted and only clearing a small path. I rested a bit and then went out to the garage and started the snowblower, fully determined to conquer this new part of my life. I managed to clear the first twelve inches off the driveway. It was a small victory, and I imagined Bill watching over me from heaven, laughing at me since I had on his *"Fargo* hat." He loved this hat since he was losing more hair each year, but I teased him, telling him he looked ridiculous with it on. I never thought that I would keep it, much less wear it.

I imagined him shaking his head at me wearing the hat, but smiling at my accomplishment. Granted, this ended up being a slightly painful victory with me on the couch the next few days with the heating pad. My muscles were just complaining about the intense use. I thought about how much I wished Bill were here, taking care of the snow and his princesses. I wept bitter tears. Oh, how I wished that he were here to comfort me and hold me! I've never felt so bereft in all my life. I missed his hugs so desperately and wanted him right there, with me, on the couch.

I miss you, my love! I do love the warmth of your Fargo hat, thanks for leaving it with me. It makes me think of you taking care of me.

> Can you fathom the mysteries of God? Can you probe the limits of the Almighty? They are higher than the heavens—what can you do? They are deeper than the depths of the grave.
>
> —Job 11:7-8

My dad flew up from Florida a few days after the snow-blowing incident to help me with the completion of the basement plan. He decided to stay until the milestone event of one year. On April 29, 2018, I would face the one-year mark of becoming a widow; Kristen would face the first year without her beloved dad. My friends were coming over that Sunday to help move boxes out of the basement into the new garage storage shelves that were put up by my dad, my brother, and my nephew, and another celebration of Bill's life. I was expecting it to be a painfully emotional day of loss.

Oh, Bill. I can't believe you have been gone for a year! I still miss you! I am getting stronger emotionally, but I have my moments of missing you to the moon and back! I know I always will.

My Borrowed Antics

KELLEY AND BRETT DROVE DOWN AND STAYED THE NIGHT BEFORE. I decided that since it was Sunday, and in typical Bill fashion, I would wake up the household to music. I smiled with Bill-type joy at the thought of doing this. He would have been in his glory, loving every minute of the musical wake-up call. I ended up crying through all the music that I played in his memory. Kelley was the first one to get up and comfort me, talking about Bill. Soon everyone was up and ready for this milestone day.

There were a few tears, a lot of work, burgers and brats on the grill. It was a tough day, but Kristen and I were surrounded by a web of love to help us through. I firmly felt my life was changing—again. This was a big milestone for this widow, and for the first time since his death, I felt a sense of optimism and a level of joy that I had not felt for a year. My chest was not so tight, finally. Easier to breathe—for today.

BILL & CHRIS SCHNEIDER, 2015

But the fruit of the Spirit is love, joy, peace, patience, kindness, goodness, faithfulness, gentleness and self-control. Against such things there is no law.

—Galatians 5:22–23

C. B. SCHNEIDER

Month Thirteen

THE PLAN FOR THE BASEMENT WAS NOW IN PLACE; WE WERE BUILDING a "mother-in-law apartment" downstairs. This was going to provide me with help to pay the house payment and give Kristen her own space for as long as she wanted to live with me. I would obtain another room to use as my office instead of having my desk or workspace out in the main living area or in my bedroom. Neither area was great for any type of work. I was excited for the construction to begin and the space to be done—for both of us. This would continue to allow both of us to move forward in this life. I couldn't wait to have a dedicated office space! We were both learning to breathe again—a little deeper now.

Early in May, I felt compelled to contact one of my friends that I have known since fourth grade, Kara. I sent her a text, telling her I really need to see her and talk to her. In my quest for solitude, I had shut her (and many others) out of my first year of widowhood. I explained that I had done this to a number of people; it hadn't been personal at all. I just hadn't known what I needed from anyone and hadn't known how to talk to anyone anyway. I had been too much of a mess back then with the physical pain. I just hadn't been able to think straight, and I hadn't wanted too many people seeing me that way. The concern had been that they would think I was losing my mind. I just had needed time to work through my loss and pain.

Little did I know that my reason for reaching out, other than seeing her after so long, was that we had a car on hand that could be fixed, and she needed a car. God again. He plans for things that his people are praying for and fulfills the prayers of his believers. Gone was my husband-handyman and fixer of all things car or computer. This meeting was a huge blessing for all involved, and I was thankful that God had plans that provided for all His children.

I now marked each day in month thirteen by writing until I could write no more. My word vomit was finally functional. I truly believed that this journey was about taking the time to think through and write about what it had meant to be a digital-age widow during the first year. There were things that I had not completed—such as shutting down Bill's emails. I had it written down on my list of widow tasks, but it was not as important as all of the other things that I had accomplished this year. Right now, chronicling my journey was the most important action I could take, other than continuing to take care of myself, my daughter, and Frodo. I had to look for a job, but this too shall have been in accordance with the plan God had for me in this widowed life.

As for the rest of my life, I just don't know right now. I am open to the constant changes that widowhood will bring my way. What I will be doing a year from now? I honestly don't know. All I know is that I have made it through the first year, despite the pain, both emotional and physical, and all the life events and upheavals that I have experienced. I am stronger because of what has happened to me. I will always miss Bill and the life that I thought we would have together as we aged (I miss his shenanigans, but WWBD is what I need to think of now). I know he watches over me from above; I feel his presence when I am sad and need it most. I just wish he could clearly direct me when it comes to some things around the house and technical issues.

As for a job, the search continues. I am open to what God has planned for me, and I will not be worried. He's got this. He is the one with the plan, and I need to be the obedient servant, like my husband was always. All I can do is continue to pray for my path to be opened and my footsteps sure. I know I will see Bill one day, and I plan to hold onto him for quite a while. I will then know what the life lesson was all about, being a digital-age widow. I can breathe now. Deeply.

Who knows? Maybe the entire goal was to sit down and write what happened to me and help someone else. If that's the case, I can accept this as my cross to bear. This thought will have to be enough to remind me to "Live Like That."

> Have I not commanded you? Be strong and courageous. Do not be terrified; do not be discouraged, for the Lord your God will be with you wherever you go.
> —Joshua 1:9

VIEW FROM MY NEW HOME OFFICE, 2018

C. B. SCHNEIDER

Afterword

I LOVE YOU, BILL. I ALWAYS WILL. YOU WERE THE BEST PART OF MY LIFE, AND I will miss you until I see you again.

Love,
Chris

Bibliography

Hope for Widows Foundation—www.hope4widows.org

MercyMe. "I Can Only Imagine." *Almost There.* Essential Music Corporation. 2001. CD.

Sidewalk Prophets. "Live Like That." *Live Like That.* Word Entertainment LLC, A Curb Company. Warner Chapel, 2012. CD.

National Suicide Prevention Lifeline (NSPL) 1800-273-TALK (8255)

International Bible Society, The Ryrie Study Bible, 1986. By The Moody Bible Institute of Chicago. The Holy Bible, New International Version Copyright 1973, 1978, 1984.

The Serenity Prayer. Reinhold Niebuhr, 1892-1971. As found on the World Wide Web at: https://en.wikipedia.org/wiki/Serenity_Prayer.

Digital Age Widow – www.digitalagewidow.com

Appendix

I Can Only Imagine

I can only imagine what it will be like
When I walk by Your side
I can only imagine what my eyes will see
When Your face is before me
I can only imagine
Yeah

Surrounded by Your glory
What will my heart feel?
Will I dance for You Jesus?
Or in awe of You be still?

Will I stand in Your presence
Or to my knees will I fall?
Will I sing, Hallelujah?
Will I be able to speak at all?
I can only imagine
I can only imagine

I can only imagine when that day comes
And I find myself standing in the sun
I can only imagine when all I will do
Is forever, forever worship You
I can only imagine, yeah
I can only imagine

Surrounded by Your glory
What will my heart feel?
Will I dance for You Jesus?
Or in awe of You be still?
Will I stand in Your presence
Or to my knees will I fall?
Will I sing, Hallelujah?
Will I be able to speak at all?
I can only imagine
I can only imagine
Surrounded by Your glory
What will my heart feel?
Will I dance for You Jesus?
Or in awe of You be still?

Will I stand in Your presence
Or to my knees will I fall?
Will I sing, Hallelujah?
Will I be able to speak at all?
I can only imagine, yeah
I can only imagine

I can only imagine, yeah
I can only imagine
I can only imagine
I can only imagine

I can only imagine
When all I would do
Is forever, forever worship You
I can only imagine

Live Like That

Sometimes I think
What will people say of me
When I'm only just a memory
When I'm home where my soul belongs

Was I love
When no one else would show up
Was I Jesus to the least of those
Was my worship more than just a song

I wanna to live like that
And give it all I have
So that everything I say and do
Points to You

If love is who I am
Then this is where I'll stand
Recklessly abandoned
Never holding back

I wanna to live like that

Am I proof
That You are who you say You are
That grace can really change a heart
Do I live like Your love is true

People pass
And even if they don't know my name
Is there evidence that I've been changed
When they see me, do they see You

I wanna to live like that
And give it all I have
So that everything I say and do
Points to You

If love is who I am
Then this is where I'll stand
Recklessly abandoned
Never holding back

I wanna to live like that

I want to show the world the love You gave for me
I'm longing for the world to know the glory of the King

I wanna to live like that
And give it all I have
So that everything I say and do
Points to You

If love is who I am
Then this is where I'll stand
Recklessly abandoned
Never holding back

I wanna to live like that

Death Discussion Checklist

THIS IS A LIST OF THINGS THAT YOU CAN USE TO DOCUMENT YOUR wishes—for both of you. If you do not have a will or estate document, this is something that you both can do for each other. Fill this out, share it with each other, make sure you both understand each other's wishes, and save it in a lockbox or safe. Update this as your life changes with time.

If you have someone that you want to provide this information to, ask them to read it, save it, and help the survivor to perform the tasks needed herein.

1. **If I should die before you, here is what I want you to be able to do for me:**
   a. If I have machines keeping me alive, then I want you to ____.
   b. If there is no chance for me to live a productive life, then I want you to ____.
   c. Celebrate my life with happiness despite how sad you will be. Ask for help in all things! People have skills in their wheelhouse that they will be happy to share with you.
   d. I am a donor; please do your best to talk to the donor foundation the day I die. I know this will be a difficult phone call, but I believe in helping

others to live a better life. Do your best! This is all that I will ever ask of you.

e. Once the donor piece is done, please deliver me to the funeral home that you have selected.

f. If possible, allow for an open casket for family and friends to be able to say goodbye to me.

g. Please have me buried or cremated.

h. If cremated, please keep my ashes with you, if this makes you happy.

i. If you wish to spread my ashes, then I would like you to do the following:

j. If you want to do something different with my ashes, you are free to do what you prefer.

2. **Please donate my clothes and personal belongings that you do not want to keep.** Please allow others to be able to reuse the items I no longer need. You know how much this made me happy in our life. If someone asks you for something, please give it to them, if you can.

a. Donate or give things away when you feel it is the right time. There is no rush to do this!

3. **I would like to give the following items to the following people:**

a. Jewelry—to our daughter or son for the future.

b. Wedding ring(s)—this is your decision. You can keep it or give it to our daughter or son when she or he is ready. Allow her or him to do whatever she or he wishes with the ring; even if this means she or he will redesign it for herself, or when she or he wants to get married. Hold onto it if she or he asks.

    c. Books—please allow family and friends to select whatever they want. Give the rest away if you want to or need to.

    d. Car—please do what you need to with this. Pay it off, give it away, donate it, or keep it for a spare.

    e. Stuff/knickknacks—please allow family and friends to select something that you don't want in your new life. I know this sounds weird, but there might be something that I have that someone else really wants to remember me by. (Even writing this sounds pretty weird.)

4. **Sell the house if you need to/move.** If there are too many memories there and you fell as if you can't move forward, then sell it. Move somewhere in which you can create new memories.

5. **I want you to move forward with your life.** I know you will mourn, and you need to take whatever time you need.

    a. Please find love again. I don't want you to be alone. I know this will be hard, but you are an amazing person who should be loved, as I have loved you.

6. **If I forgot to list something here, please use your best judgment on what should be done.**

    a. I love you and trust that you will be able to do what you believe is right to honor my memory.